Her Strange Angels

Sarah La Rosa

xo,
Sarah LaRosa

For my mother,

my first encounter

with Divine Love

on this side.

Not I, not I, but the wind that blows through me!
A fine wind is blowing the new direction of
Time.
If only I let it bear me, carry me, if only it carry
me!
If only I am sensitive, subtle, oh, delicate, a
winged gift!
If only, most lovely of all, I yield myself and am
borrowed
By the fine, fine wind that takes its course
though the chaos of the world
Like a fine, an exquisite chisel, a wedge-blade
inserted;
If only I am keen and hard like the sheer tip of a
wedge
Driven by invisible blows,
The rock will split, we shall come at the wonder,
we shall find the Hesperides.
Oh, for the wonder that bubbles into my soul,
I would be a good fountain, a good well-head,
Would blur no whisper, spoil no expression.
What is the knocking?
What is the knocking at the door in the night?
It is somebody wants to do us harm.
No, no, it is the three strange angels.
Admit them, admit them.

- D.H. Lawrence

Contents: The Many Gifts of Strange Angels

Introduction

I was the little girl who dreamed of being a writer.

I tortured my brothers and sisters throughout our childhood, and into my teens, with stories of great romances, magic, and even ventured into comedic glory. I cajoled and coerced them into my room, shutting the door. I made them sit and listen to me as I read fabulous work and played almost-as-fabulous music I'd selected for soundtracks, to lend extra emotion.

I was committed.

They rolled their eyes, barely tolerating my urgent creative brilliance. They'd eventually escape the prison of my room by resorting to loud outbursts of frustration, or yelling "Mom!!" hoping for salvation.

Bless my mother.

She held the balance between rescuing her other children from my handwritten dramas, and listening with devoted attention to my ideas and use of *way* too many adjectives.

She gave me constructive feedback on every single story I bombarded her with.

Somehow, with an ever-increasing number of children to herd (she would eventually have eight), lesson plans for different grade levels (she homeschooled us), meals to prepare, a home to keep, little to no income so much of the time, and never any security in our housing, my mother managed to make my little stories something important to her. She never allowed me to feel that I was wasting her time, exhausting her, or pursuing anything other than my true and rightful destiny.

When I was 14 years old, she told me that I had a gift for *imagery*. I pretended in that moment to know exactly what she meant, being the sage I was, but I had no idea. So at the very first chance I snuck off and looked that word up in the dictionary: *IMAGERY*.

I was thrilled to discover that my mother believed I had the ability to retrieve ideas and use words to create vivid pictures of them.

The idea was electric, and sent a jolt through my chest. That moment was my first taste of magic, and I wanted more.

While I've left behind the melodramatic stories of my childhood and teens (you're welcome), words have not left me. I write because I must. Writing is a practice that brings me, reliably, into the presence of the divine.
Most of what I scribble into my journals, on random notebook paper, or into the notes app of my phone is what I would consider inconsequential.

But sometimes, something takes over, and a strange angel appears on the page, or at the window, or comes rushing through my window riding a sudden gust of wind that lifts the drapes, and the hair from my face.

In those moments, holiness is a tangible thing. The air around me takes on a near smokiness; a haze where spirit abides to whisper secret gems that drop into my hands and mouth.

Too often, I can only write fast enough to capture and relate a portion of what I sense, before it is gone and I am alone with my words in a still room, ordinary once more.

Happily, I have discovered that these strange angels, as D.H. Lawrence speaks of them in his glorious poem, can be seen and spoken with in the many dark and frightening seasons of our life, as well as the very ordinary hours we pass day to day.

These angels confer sacraments upon us-
"…visible signs of an inward grace",
as the definition declares.

Her Strange Angels is nearly six years' worth of writing that came directly from that sort of experience- communion with strange angels, or spirit, or God- as you like. Moments of quiet contentment, hidden inside seasons of chaos and upheaval. One sweet, deep breath in the midst of lung-searing sobs as I left relationships, jobs, cities, expectations and dreams behind-or was left by them.

A sudden, unexpected glimpse of what is eternal in the middle of a very long, ordinary, tiring day chasing a toddler around. One perfect meal, served at the exact perfect time- healing beyond words. A gentle, precious embrace by some invisible source when feelings of isolation and hopelessness threatened to suffocate.

All these gifts, and they are gifts more precious than we can ever know, come to us constantly-relentlessly even. Spirit never quits. We are Priority Number One. Our obstacle is entirely self-made. We do not see the angels descending and ascending our very own Jacob's ladder in the night sky before us because we are so deeply focused on our pain, our expectations, and our demands. A veil sits over our eyes, shielding us from the healing beauty we sit inside and smothering the light that permeates our lives.

But for those willing to part the veil, mysteries and gracious gifts ABOUND. Sacraments. Visible signs of an inward grace imparted to us from the cosmos. And what is grace, but a sacred container designed to hold us intact as we keep moving, keep loving, keep parenting, working, cleaning, cooking, writing, playing, creating, BE-ing in this physical world with vast, rarefied longings toward a home we sense, but do not see.

Words well spun can sometimes part the veil, or at least help us to remember *we* can. It is my deepest prayer that you find words in these pages that will help you remember.

If and when you do, make them yours, call forth whatever power they summon in you, and unlock the front door. Angels are at your gate.

Blessings on you,
Sarah

Recognition

Welcome home, Beloved.

You are safe here
among the wreckage
of grand plans gone awry
slowly awakening
to the Great Mystery
of your own life
your own brilliance
your own destiny.

Embrace the chaos
of unknowing.

Inside those murky depths
is your place
your time
your purpose.

Debris

Those stones and shells
are yesterday's residue.

What washes up
on today's tide
is as yet
unknown to me.

Whatever it may be
in whatever form it takes
I can be assured
it is meant for me.

Mermaids

The way to find a measure of solace
in the place of unknowing
of waiting
on the verge
of deep waters
is to remember
that we are equipped
with ability to float.

Water is our natural state.

We had our beginnings
in a sacred sea
and so returning
to that vast ocean
does not have to be scary
and unknown.

It could be more like going home.

Flying Lessons

I have come too far
have grown wings
have gained a new night vision
that allows me to peer
into the beauty of dark places
that frighten others.

I will not return to the old life.

I cannot.

The air is too sweet up here
and with each passing mile of flight
I become bolder
hungrier
faster.

Runaway

I retain faint memories
of my life in captivity.

I can feel at times
the phantom pains
of amputated fears
and beliefs
still clinging
to parts of my brain
that remember
who I used to be
or
who I used to think I was.

But they are not me
nor have they ever been.

I am smarter now
braver now
with years and some distance
I have adopted a courage
that propels me
into speaking
my own truth
and I am not ashamed
when my voice quivers
a bit.

I am still learning
what it means to sing.

Skin

Vulnerable
is a four-letter word.

Exposed
is a profanity
until I remember
that god dwells there
in her nakedness.

And then I remember
they are sacraments.

Fluency

There are no sounds
that adequately contain
the potency of soul-speak.

Our efforts are mere attempts
at articulating something
so vast and eternal within us
that we can never write it or speak it
wholly.

It can only be felt wholly
in the body, in the heart
in the dark.

We convey these soul truths
through our stories-
the ones about ourselves
about our mothers
our mothers' mothers.

Our stories are an embroidery
of blood and broken bread.

Our language itself
a shapeshifting power
only we can wield
only we can recognize
in another's mother tongue.

We speak it to ourselves
in silence
in writing
in art
in sacred movement
in listening deeply.

The words change and morph
but there is a fragrance
that attaches itself
and we recognize
the memory of scent
that pulls us back
to innocence and trust
back to womb space.

And we lose it along the way.

Or we are forbidden to speak it.

Or it is stolen.

We take up The Language of The Captive.
We teach our children to speak
only the words of the conquerors
imitating their gestures, inflections
and intonations.

We pretend that we don't remember
who we are
who we always were.

Beloved, don't be afraid.
Don't be ashamed.

It always returns to remind you.
It will not go away forever.

SHE cannot be suppressed forever.

Her words, Her language
weave their way back
in ways so skillful
and sometimes so subtly
that you do not realize
you have remembered
until you are speaking fluently
the language you forgot
you always knew.

And sometimes
the return to the knowledge
of your native tongue
is so sharp and explosive
that the words split you
from the inside out
a boulder cracked and hewn
by soul-waters gushing forth
from a deeper well
that has slowly filled
with the passing months and years
to overflowing
bursting the old containers
that no longer fit your wild self
freed at last.

This native tongue
sounds like groanings
of new mothers
who share the burden of new life
pushing its way through to the light.

It is the language of birdsong
not only the chirp and trill
but the squawk and caw
the screech and howl.

The soul is unconcerned
whether your words are elegant
but only that you speak them.

Our language has one requirement:
speak it, lest it die.

How we choose to become fluent
is our personal business.

That we do
is the single most important task
along our path.

May you choose fluency.
May you give voice
to your native tongue.

May our Great Mother
in Her Wisdom
infuse your body and heart
with the courage
to begin practicing
new words of wildness
that you may be recognized
in your natural habitat.

A Wild Shadow

She lurks in the Wild Longing Place
of the heart
listening for the exact right moment
to pounce.

She is a lioness
who has had enough
of being cornered.

She will slink and slither
through the most dense of forests
in search of the predator
that has relentlessly stalked Her den.

She will lay hold of the lies
and she will tear them apart
one by one by one.

She will not leave the fresh kill
until you observe it
look it full in the face
and recognize
that what you see lying there
was never you.

This is the one that belongs with you
She is mighty
She is a dark mother
a murder of crows
a shapeshifting sister
who calls on a creative fire inside you
transforming you.

Incense

Let it weave through you
moving into your caverns and caves
smoke filling your lungs
with the sweetest fragrance
tinged with the damp you know
always accompanies truth.

You are meant for the sunlight
and you are meant for the dark.

The Call

Answering The Call is to turn
to a new path
to begin moving another direction
usually into darkening forests
whose trails are narrow and obscured.

Contained within The Call
is the imperative to walk away
from what is currently before you:
the leave-taking of a previous path
to wander, seemingly aimlessly at times
a wooded night.

There may be others
on that current path with you.

They stare as you move away.

Some are stunned, or angry.

Some shake their head
in disappointment or fear
for the loss of your presence
and agreement.

As you move away
from the company of
Those Who Think Like Me
you begin to realize that
you haven't thought like them
for some time now.

The thought of continuing on
as you have for so long
is causing such a rift
that it threatens to divide you
from your very essence.

If you don't finally answer this time
The Call may never come to you again.

You can't risk that possibility.

So you begin to trudge
through poison oak
nettles and briar patches
scratched and scraped
tired and thirsty.

There is no room at the inn.
You are called to the Wild Wood
and there you will remain
because you know that
only in those wild places
will you finally come upon
what you have always searched for.

To answer The Call
is to change your name
releasing the syllables and sounds
of your former self
to adopt your rightful title.

You are no longer
Compliance
Prudence
Chastity.

Your identity is finally stripped down
to only what is real
your new oldest name:
Wildish

and your handwriting is scrawling
fast and recognizable only to those
who write the same way.

You stop trying to write beautifully
and begin writing what is true.

The Call demands this of you.

It is a growing pain
that begins at the center
and radiates outward
to singe and burn away
everything it touches that cannot last.

This is the very nature of metamorphosis.

For the shedding of skin
into a new being
is intrinsically painful.

I have stopped trying to avoid pain.

What remains is strong
resilient
and worthy.

Everything else
is a skin fit for then
and we can find the courage
to let it go
in favor of now.

Along the way
you will meet up with sisters
who have answered their own call.

After years of trudging alone
to the single note of our own call
we begin to sense first
then to recognize
their dirt-smudged, tear-streaked faces.

Their scars look comfortingly similar
to our own.

We are a ragtag tribe of outcasts
moon howling, spiritual homesteaders.

The notes of our own call
begin to merge and blend
and we become
a symphony of stragglers
circling in sacred ritual
we are never truly alone.

Our wounds are treasure maps
tracing our stories back
to the moment we said no
enough
no more
now
this time.

They bind us
these wounds, these calls
one to another
on this dark wooded path.

To answer The Call is to choose
a life outside
what anyone else deems worthy.

We are heralded by some
as over emotional
ridiculous
dramatic
eccentric
strange
weird
unnatural.

Others like us
will recognize themselves
in our journey
our words
our artwork
our altars
our homegrown vegetables
and homespun clothes.

They will feel they are home
when they smell lavender at our neck
and see sage on our tables.

Our legacy is red
and burns with a passion we cannot contain
so that it seeps out and stains
our daughters and sons
marking them
for a new way of life that emerges
because we were brave enough
to answer a Call.

Starlight

There is that painful shift in awareness.

You sit, lumpy and listless
in a seat you've outgrown.

You see before you a new territory
the place you reach for
and long to walk toward.

And there is the space between.

Transient stars
busy forming new life
burning out and dying
darkening
before a new incarnation.

Allow the blank spaces
between lines
the time between time
the indigo breaths
before the beginning.

Soften the gaze
to let what must pass
pass.

Forgo grasping
what is dissolving
and understand
that in the departure
is both the liberation
of new movements
and the right
more, imperative
to dance them.

Creative expression of the divine
rests
in a perpetual motion
a constant birthing
and deathing revolution.

Nothing remains
save the dance of dark and light.

This is flux
this is the dynamic of life
the rush of waters
the beating of wings
the pilgrimage of restless stars.

The Nothing

Dark water
muddy water
groundwater
Creativity is like this
swirling
and circling
and thick.

There is no easy, clear flow
of sparkling oceans and singing rivers.

My muse comes to me in the mud-
that sacred mixture:
dirt and dark water
that heals blind eyes
and draws toxins
from the skin and deeper organs.

The smell is pungent.

This is the artery of the earth
this is the tar-colored pitch
that feeds the tributaries
flowing toward La Loba who gathers
to Kali who destroys
to the truths I'd rather avoid
inside of myself
about myself
in spite of myself.

One has no choice
but to face the Great Nothing
if one is to find
the Underneath River.

It is a gift, the nothing.

It empties us utterly
of falsity and the hollow stubbornness
that claims to be abiding strength of spirit
but drains us of genuine courage instead.

And we must be emptied
if we are to be fed the living water of spirit.

And so, what is one to do?

What is the solution
the course of action
while stranded in the desert?

Do you sit to conserve your strength
praying that you live
through this painful dehydration
of the soul?

No.

Continue on
feel the burning sand
between your toes
feel yourself melting
and merging
with the Great Nothing.

Sink
below
dunes and heat.

There you will find
a cool, dark place
that smells of ancient rains
collected on the ground
beneath your blistered feet.

The waters rise.

Wilderlings

It is a paradox-
a wild thing that heals a domesticated heart.

Or perhaps it only feels like a paradox
because of the years we have been taught
to fear what is wild
what is uncontrollable
by those who fear her.

To return to the Wild
is to go home
to the only home
you've ever really known
in your deepest soul-self.

There are treasures for you there
they've been waiting
as patiently as wild things are able
which is not very much.

This is the stamping in your gut
the pawing at the ground
the straining of your neck
reaching to see over the next hill
that next ridge line
to the next horizon.

There is no need to look so.

No need to strain yourself
staring at horizons.

Look to the earth.

Wildness marks your path
with a winged trail.

If nothing else-
to remind you of your winged self
and to provide the means of flight
one dropped feather at a time.

Gather them all.

Sew them to your heart.

Re-member your Wild Self.

Dark Harbingers

There is good news.
That little voice inside
(that isn't all that little)
continues to kick up a ruckus.

The crow keeps up her cawing
waking you from your semi-comatose sleep
until you throw back the covers
to see what all the fuss is about.

She's there
sitting on the fence post
outside your back window
a little worse for the wear
perhaps a bit pecked
she always was a bit too loud
to fit in with the rest.

But you know her.

She is yours.

Claim her.

Let her remind you
of what you forgot.

She is a harbinger
of darkness, that's true.

But you've always known her secret-
she is the way to your true home
to wolfish ways
and a pack that recognizes you
as sister-
lumps, cackle and all.

Severance

Go home to Nike.

A little bird told me
to pay attention.

There are no coincidences.

All these happenings
all these dreams
all these small serendipities
are the voice of the Winged One
who faces west to the sea and the sunset
to the ebb and flow
to our change and our stasis.

The famous Winged Victory of Samothrace-
the most famous Winged Victory in the
world
is severed.

Was she made that way?
Did conquerors, time or the elements
take from her lovely being
face, brain and intellect?
She has lost her head
lost her mind.

What remains:
heart
breast
legs
and wings.

She is instinct and action
She is bosom and belly
She is a torn off wing clutched in a talon
She is flight without the over-analysis
of too linear mind
She is the goddess of Do It
Done It
Not: think about it, worry over it, belabor it,
chew it flavorless
and beat it to death.

She is primordial.

Wing first, think later.

In her lack lies her potency.

She stands solid at the prow
of a long destroyed ship.

Leaning into the wind
riding the current
of that river beneath the river
daughter of Styx.

She is both wing and wind.

I hear her voice in the song of birds
finches and hawks, jays and crows.

Warbling, cawing, screeching sounds
that populate the hours between dawn and
dusk.

The sound of beating and flapping wings.

She is the mother of ugly ducklings
who do not yet know themselves.

They see only severed bits
of yearned-for futures.

White swan wings lift into the air
there is a glimmer of recognition
and we have a glimpse
a taste
the faintest intuition
that we belong in those same skies.

I see her fingers in the wind
that brush the treetops
that ruffle feathers
and stir up still air.

To go home to Nike
I am taking stock of all my moving parts
hands and head, legs and heart.

To be whole, to be winged
requires insane trust
in the instincts of Self.

She tells me to pay attention
to these bloodied, dismembered wings
I come across.

Victory looks like a remembering.

We may be a patchwork of wings
and woman parts
but we will be whole
and there is nothing more beautiful
after lifetimes of brokenness.

The Art of Becoming

And what of knowing?

And what of certainties, and guarantees
and the deep comfort that comes
with full disclosure?

This is not meant.

I am destined for numinous clouds
containing maybes and sort ofs
and perhapses.

Releasing the death grip on black and white
means I embrace the murkier shades
that cannot be qualified, categorized
summarized and counted.

Instead, I am gifted with a freedom of
movement
inside large gray spaces
free to follow my intuition
free to follow my soul
free to follow in the pathway
of the divine footstep.

Even the shape of that footprint
changes
one minute a wolf pawing her way
toward a babbling brook
the next a set of sharp talon scratches
that lift off into a mist
flying so far and fast
that I am lost
in her foggy trail.

To undulate, to transform, to evolve
to BECOME, to step over the next threshold
the darker portal, down the lower steps
through the heavier door
into the damp cave spaces
where I lose my body
absorbed into the darkness
becoming the moist air
the cool staleness of breaths
that have remained
a million generations
waiting for me
lingering only to offer up their secrets
to me.

Their secrets
replace my circulatory system
their little breezes
take over the open areas
that made up my mouth and ears and eyes.

I am refashioned
into a creature
ten million years old
ancient, wise, unattached
to my skin, my face, my tongue.

Their old knowings
revealed in my now self
opening a vast sea span
of water wisdoms
whose words
forever begin and end
with Let Go.

I reach for handfuls of saltwater
trying desperately to hold
what is filling my fingers
watching it ebb gleefully
back to its rightful home
its natural state of grace.

This mad collection of raindrops dance and
sing
of beauty and peace and the dark blue
revelation
of eternity surrounding my body.

Thrashing around
I displace more than I drink
wasting my energy in permanence
draining my heart
in the craving for solidity.

The past hurt, the present struggle
and the fear of the future mingles, mixes
and becomes a new being

one giant shriek in my throat

pummeling me
with threats of failure
of inadequacy
of what must be.

I let out a howl
a tearing hysterical sob
meant to vocalize my protest.

Instead it rips open the wanting place
liberating words that fly with beating wings
escaping through every crack they can find
widening each opening until my soul is laid
bare
as a canyon
thirsty and ready to be filled.

Let Go
let go
let go...

The breaths and the breezes and the
raindrops falling to the sea
say a chant repeated
over and over in my body
uncurl your fingers, open your hands
spread your arms wide.

They move in spirals inside my ears
where they took up residence so recently.

Moisture collects on and under my tongue
a sublingual rainfall
where the words of elders sit
comfortable and wrinkled
waiting
waiting for me to recognize them.

Shifting gray mist moves past my eyes
and my sight is the sight of those
who have always come before
as I will go before those coming after me
into caves
swimming in dark blue seas
standing in cooling rainstorms
at the edge of canyons.

Here, I am supported by something invisible
from behind.

The sensation of safety finally reaches me
from a source unknown
but I can feel the rhythmic push of air
at my back
and I can see the shadow of feathered arms.

Omens

The sea, air, moon, crows, coyotes and night
all conspire to speak to me
in a language my brain resists
through its ignorance and worship
of progress
but that my heart intuitively understands
in spirals.

I move from one epiphany of grace
to the next
and each is just enough
to sustain me
until I have need of another.

Sea Legs

I come to the sea
when I know it is time to let go.

There is no such thing as grasping here.

There is only letting go
or drown.

And so the sea calls me frequently
and calls
and calls
and will not stop calling
until I've discovered my body
slowly hardening from the feet up
a sandy cement forming from the outside in
that only ocean water dissolves.

Once freed
I am released
to float to the bottom
quite naturally
coming to quiet rest
on the ocean floor
to be still and sucked underground
to darker dirt
and the waiting container
of my transformation.

I feel gravity more strongly now
as if the earth herself
is heavier
weightier under my feet
and my blood along with it.

The sea teaches me
wisdoms
of perpetual motion
and the necessity of my undoing.

I sit with the contradiction:
the ceaseless ebb and flow of waters
and the stillness of black earth
beneath me.

Both pull me under
both are containers for new life
and both facilitate
the slow moving descent necessary
to reach it.

Baptism

What is your name?

Do you remember it?

Can you recall the sound
the feel of fingertips in your chest
as it gripped your heart as a child?

And what is the name of your god?

You drew the letters in the dust
when you thought nobody saw you
bending skinned knees made raw
from climbing rough barked trees
scraped elbows
hinged
as your fingers scrawled the word
on your skin
and on your tongue
and in your mind
an oracle unknown.

A chant, a song, a prayer
oh god, let this be me, you'd beg
with every muscle in your small child body.

To fly!

To swim fish-tailed and free
to sit on a throne of crystal
to mix potions and wave a willow wand
you knew this was your birthright.

You'd been misplaced, is all.

And now
can you feel the fire begin
in the marrow of your bones?

A spinning slowly at first
licking searing slippery heat at your neck
swirling faster and faster
until you streak up into the sky
a screaming firecracker
a sparkler
a shooting star in reverse
finding your place
among a million watt night sky.

Not so fast
the earth pulls you back down
gravity your dark sister
yanking feet, calves
skinned knees both.

You are MINE, she cackles
and her unpretty laugh
is your laugh too.

Cool earth, warm earth, damp earth
pulling you to your beginning
this is where I began
this is where I start
you hear the bones say.

The sounds
are sounds of silence
of burials
of worm dances.

And a river moves.
Under.

Black water leeches away the soil
that enfolded your dirt made body
and you are mobile once more
as waves stir your arms
teaching you movements
you forgot you knew.

This is how you write your name, they say.

They lap secret letters into the canal of your
ear
and the sounds are the sounds
of crying, singing, of finding
things once thought lost
forever.

Now,
water whispers.

A voice
that seems to originate in your belly
speaks a word that repeats
A relentless invocation
until you know
you will never again forget your name.

This is birthright.
Blood rite.

There is a fierce calling-to in the blood
that yearns toward fullness.

Any unattended corner of the soul
left in open emptiness
craves the satisfaction that comes
with the knowing of one's name.

One's true name
given before the edges of time and space
the name that sleeps
restlessly in the bones
awaiting the release that comes
with soul wakening.

The utterance of such a name is heard
in the sounds of hyenas
closing in for the kill.

It is heard in the laughter of old women
who already know the joke
the bark-like warning of a doe to her fawn
and a thousand other oracles
living secret, magical lives
in our very midst.

We scratch away the filmy residue
that hides the spirit world from our vision
when we take up creative flame in our hand
and begin once more
drawing letters in the dust.

We name our gods
as we name ourselves
by way of trials
ecstasies
grief.

A spirituality
that does not live
in our body
does not live.

Our gods must be rooted
in the same soil our feet and fingernails are
dirty with the planting
scented in sweat
soft in the womb.

A god lives
that is both mother as well as father
sister and brother
child and self.

A god lives
that is remembered
in the blood
and the bone
of a human container.

We see our own name
and that of our gods
in the call of wild things
that perch, leap and tear
through underbrush
toward throbbing, pulsing life.

Taking it in
we are remembered
we are made whole
and our name comes back to us
from the four directions.

Our name was scattered
and sent to those places
to be held in safe keeping
until we were able to perceive it once more
to be trusted with the sacred responsibility
that comes with knowing one's name.

Do you remember?

Coyote Medicine

Don't make the mistake
of dismissing that vibrating ambivalence
seated firmly inside you.

She's been prowling around your chakras
looking to pick a fight.
The kind of fight you were woven together
and destined to win.

And in the quest for victory
you will discover
that you are inhabited by friend
not foe.

All that foul-smelling disillusionment
surrounding you
is not your failure, your inadequacy
your worthlessness.

No, dear one
it's Coyote dancing in circles
around your fuzzy brain
tricking you, teasing mercilessly
as Coyote does.

Creator, jester, cackle and growl
taking little nibbles from your flesh
while you spin around
wondering if you're losing your mind.

A holy frustration descends
until you want to grab hanks of your own
hair
and bellow to the vast skies.

Go ahead.

Your howl
is the howl
of Coyote.

She's stepped in a briar patch
and lodged thorns in her paw.

In search of sacred wells of wisdom
she's just spent days
no weeks
trying to chase down a mirage
lapping on heat waves at a distant horizon.

And all this chaos is as it should be.

This is the dance of the soul
as it prepares for an unfolding
a revelation
the last wobbling, reticent steps
before you realize
you're already through that door
and over the threshold.

From chaos, order.
From the great void, illumination.

What you need to do next
comes in a way that opens so naturally
you wonder that you did not see it there
always.

This howling, holy, sacred frustration
is what propels us out of our complacency.
We yearn.
We strive.
We long for the aha! moment
all the while cursing the silence we sit
inside.

We suffer sleeplessness at night
and malaise in the afternoon hours
it feels as if you will go mad.

We howl.

Our own anxious inaction
becomes repulsive to us
and any fears about outcomes
become so irrelevant
as to become hilarious.

We must break through or die.

The soul will have its way
and we are carried along
slung across the shoulders
of a strong inner will.

We know too much to look away this time
and there is nothing for it
but the true source that feeds the self
the creative life.

To live a holy life
filled with many different kinds of beauty
moved by wisdom
enabled on that path by a potent grace
that suffuses and saturates limbs and eyes
the pores of the skin
seeping into a heated bloodstream
and further, to the living bone
and marrow within
this is our howling.

This is our longing.
This is our yearning.
This is the promise
for those of us willing to endure
and tightly embrace a coyote sister
and a healing dose of sacred frustration.

If there is great, chaotic frustration in the
soul
it is certain that awakening is imminent
and that one is approaching
an important transition.

Blessed are those who stand at the verge.

Blood Moon

The Blood Moon of October
rounds herself out
a pregnancy full term.

Come the morning, she will have crested
tipped over the edge
into the magic minutes of completeness
before beginning the shedding of so much
light
on her journey into the dark space of
starlight
once more.

The Blood Moon is known by other names
Harvest Moon
Hunter's Moon
Falling Leaf Moon

But I know what she is to me
and I cannot pretend it away
for the comfort of a softer name.

This is the ancient time of slaughtering.

And underneath death
is a tender pink self
unsure of her steps.

Everything is brighter, more sensitized
and so new as to be a bit terrifying.

We step into this new space
without being expert in the terrain
but moving raw, new feet
through its outer boundaries nonetheless.
Because we must.

This tender self
unskilled in the ways of grace
is stunned to find herself
in the role of novice once more.

In the old skin
so recently ripped from her body
she flowed and danced and twirled with
ease.

We have never forgotten
that this disturbing awkwardness
is where we started.

We just hoped we would never have to
return.

And now comes the rub.
We will never stop returning.

Within each shedding
of current being
is the requirement
of beginning again.

All the same rules apply:
Speak, test, try, risk, observe, fall
receive, try again, learn more, balance
almost fall again, try again, move forward.

We spend so much of our energy
working up to the letting go
to the death and release
that we are ill-prepared
for tender baby steps inside new feet.

Perhaps this is best.

There can be wisdom in tearing ahead
blissfully ignorant.

Perhaps if we remembered each time
that we would be starting over
again and again and again
we would choose stasis.

We might remain in the familiar alleyways
the already-trod-smooth paths
and never push into the next sacred spaces
that so eagerly await our arrival.

And they are eagerly awaiting our arrival,
Beloved.

Vows

The oaths we mouth boldly
to the wolves and wild places within us
are the epiphanies hard-won
through the previous shedding of older skins
and the toughening we met
in earlier pilgrimages.

These epiphanies grow and evolve
they take form in our art
our words and our creative labors.

We breathe life into them
name them, describe them
give them a voice all their own.

They are heard and intuited
by those around us
and we are healed
in the glow of their potent truths.

And now the time comes
to reach further in
to wilder places
wider spaces
through an initiation
of shedding blood and skin.

Strange Angels

What are these truths we seek
in dark sanctuaries
across numinous thresholds?

They anchor feral feet
to waiting wild lands.

Silences

In the season of descent we are faced anew
with the most tangible understanding
of silence.

Silence becomes our most holy, sacred
invocation to the spirits.

The silence of these darkening days
is not one void of sound.

Rather
it is the intentional and deliberate quieting
of our own voice
in order to hear the words of the wise ones
the ancient ones reaching out to us.

It is an acknowledgement
that we do not have the answers already
that we do not know
and that we are humble in our unknowing.

There is an exquisite loveliness
to the uncertainty we sit inside.

Within the discomfort of struggle to know
there comes a delicate and fluid dance of
soul.

There is magic in that place.
There is magic-making in that place.

Because in the discomfort of unknowing
of uncertainties
there is intrinsic silence
that opens the way.

We do not know what to say
what to write, who to call, who to be.
We just don't know.
We think we should.

Beautifully, the soul knows its footing here.

It begins the dance
that calls to magic
the magic of understanding
of opening thresholds and transformations.

We become fertile in that place.
There is a turning over of the soil in us.

As the soil is tilled and disturbed
our feet sink lower
earthing down into darkness.

We learn the wisdom
of a sacred immobility.

It is an utter lack of movement
seen in wild things ready to pounce
ready to tear flesh
ready to feed.

Before the breaking, shattering leap
the motionless observation
with ears pricked.
A hearing of the spirits
in silence.

It is in this sacred space
of unknowing silence
that holy direction is divined.

The striving ego reaches
toward an unattainable
toxic sense of perfection
that curtails the processes
of the wild, creative life.

Those processes ebb and flow
wax and wane
bellow and shush
all in turn, over and over again.

They cannot and will never
be regulated, formulated
packaged or promoted
in tidy gift boxes.
They cannot and will never
be commanded forth.

They must be summoned
in the spaces of silence
where they can be heard with the heart.

The magical life and her processes
are rhythmic, beautiful, intoxicating,
untamed.

She is a wild thing we run after
and we cannot dictate to her
what she is to be
in us or to us.

No, we can only follow her through the
thicket.

But the soul knows.
It remembers what our mind forgot.
Where memory fails, the body recalls
the sound of home, of safe direction
and the ancient voices of ancestors.

This way
we hear with an inner ear
and the words are vibrations in our heart.

It is visceral, this sensibility.

The magic that takes place
in such a silence
is felt bodily.

You know that if you turn your gaze
quickly enough
you will see the spirits moving.

They are speaking words you may only hear
in your deliberate and respectful silences.

Quietly
so quietly
tilt your head and cock your ear.
There is a voice in the air at your side.

And there it is before you- the way.

Breakthrough

There is no reusable cocoon.

Once birth has taken place
what sustained new life
in all those weeks and months
passes on, away
and is no longer necessary.

Each process
each developmental journey
is unique to the soul that traverses its
landscape.

And there are times that this hurts
feels confusing, shadowy
frighteningly impossible.

What can I possibly say
that hasn't already been said?
Who do I think I am to offer up anything at
all
outside an honorable existence?
What if I'm not good enough
quick enough, knowledgeable enough?
What if I never achieve my goal? What if I
fail? How do I even begin? How can I ever
keep pace with those around me?

These are often dark moments.

I stand at the borderlands
of a territory I have no knowledge of.
This mileage before me is wild, dangerous
land.
And yet, it is my land.
There is no other for me.

When the angels were handing out
homesteading claim flags
mine bore a number I did not recognize
and they pointed me in a direction
I did not want to go.

But that is for me
and no other plot of soil will do.

I cannot beg the soft-rubbed interior
of another's cocoon.
I cannot intrude on another's creative space
and expect that my creation will develop
organically, naturally.

It is hard to admit, most of all to myself.
But I am reluctant to leave the warmth
and safety, the known-ness of this softer
cocoon.

To dream and plot
inside the mother womb of ideas
is infinitely more comfortable.
There is no rejection here
no risk of falling
of failing.

If I never get started
I never have to risk injury
and everything remains a possibility.

But to remain in the soft, liquid spaces of
possibility forever
is to miscarry the Real
because What Is Real
demands fresh air and movement.

And so sweat and risk
become allies on this journey.

Cutting my own path
through an untamed landscape
means I have to walk
very
slowly.

In walking very slowly
I begin to notice everything.

I hear a rustle in the air at my side.
I turn to look
and there a leaf begins a slow, twirling
descent
from her branch so many feet above my
head.

Her progress is spiraling
and her dance is familiar.

She glances at me as she makes her way
to the waiting ground below
I hear her ycllowed voice as she passes by
This way, she calls.

Quickening

Like breath in the lungs
there is an unending expanding
and contracting force for life
in the seeking soul's journey.

Like Inanna
I move through inky black corridors
feeling my way
along a cool stone passageway
that thrums and throbs
with its own heartbeat.

The steps ahead are unknown to my feet
but I trust the rock under my hand.

These walls will not crush me.

A serpentine way
a labyrinth within
and the circle turns.

From this darkness
I am gifted with an abiding
and revelatory comfort.

All is well.
All is as it should be.
I am held secure
within a great womb.

In struggling to conceive my own soul truths
to incubate my thoughts and dreams
I have discovered
I am the thing incubating.

My very self is what grows and develops
in this place.
I am the cycle
the revolution of moons and days.
I am the thing quickening.

It is my arms and hands
being stitched together
in the secret place.

I am the new life being birthed
in each moment
with each step
in every breath.

And the circle turns again
becoming an entrancement
an entrance
opening to something
familiar.

I know this place.
This is where light is born.

Rosary to a Dark Mother

She is the disturber of souls
this black god mother.

My own soul instinctively
reaches out for her
like a trusting child
even as my frightened mind recoils
from her darkness
time and time again.

She permeates everything
diffuses all nighted light
penetrates every neglected crook and cranny
shining her deep blackness into our center.

She is visceral sensibility
always appropriate in her untamed wildness.

We see our desperate need for rebirth
in her waters
yet fear the unwinding at her hands
that we know is prerequisite
to glorious emergence.

She carries our fear
quite competently
and always compassionately.
We need not be terrorized.

She is The Healer of all Healers
the first and always wisewoman witch.

There is an abundance of spirit to be found
in witnessing her skilled hand
and I have found solace in her sanctuaries.

She calls me by name
and I am gratefully found.

Gathered up by her seeking spirit
from rock-strewn roads
stumbling toward her clumsily
blinded by so many glaring distractions
relieved to be taken in at last
tattered though I may be.

The very sounds of her many names
invoke a thick coating of holy
onto my tongue
and fill my mouth
with the smoke of unwritten hymns.

I say the words over and over again
the syllables of her
and feel deeper resonances descend
through my head and into my belly
a sacred planting, a recognition.

This is prayer.
I am seeded in early morning hours of
darkness.
There is the wind
the blackness of lowering wintered skies
and I in my body.
I am listening.
I am still.

I gaze into the glowing reflection of her dark
face by candlelight
gazing back at me
a challenge and an invitation.

Her silence
her stillness
is both unnerving and comforting.
A solid place to lean into
if I dare.

Those shifting shadows in my line of sight
those tongueless oracles
that speak in the presence of fog
are calling me home
to smoke-saturated sanctuaries
long forgotten
and the waiting gaze of She Who Sees Me.

I remember her.
She grows me inward and down
rather than upward and out.

She is the shapeshifting provocateur
the midnight incendiary
who edges me closer to that jagged ledge
than is comfortable.
I stare the precipice down
unsure if I am daring it or myself
to melt away.

This is the choosing of fate
under the fierce gaze
of unapologetic eyes.

She waits for me at this edge.
She always has and always will.

To cling fearfully
against these familiar crumbling walls
or lean into thin air and windward ways
this is the decision
again and again
cycle upon cycle
layer under layer.

Destruction lies ahead either way.

That is her way
to dismember, dissolve, deconstruct.

For she is both fecundity and barren lands
leeching the last drops of moisture
from desolated ground
ferocious in her thirst.

Yet her destruction is a sacred one
not reckless violence
for the sake of violence.
No.

She is tearing down every pretense
every illusion, every hidden hurt
that becomes just one more excuse
to retreat from the knowledge of Who I Am
and Who I Have Always Been
in any and all lifetimes.

The fluttering I feel at my core
is the first subtle movements of recognition
beginning to grow and take hold.

I am raw with the stretching
but so deeply filled.

I remember her now.
I remember me now.

We are the same inky blackness
the same smoky tang in the air
the same unspoken words.

This priming in the body
is both an emptying and a filling up
coming into closer contact with divine
presence
a dark mother
a holy madonna
seated in wisdom.

This is me approaching Her.

Wilder Mercies

What is left
when all the words have been spoken
all the tears shed
the full emptying out and breaking open
of every last bit of assumption
and the draining of pretended grace …

Could it be
that in this flattened state
in the blankness of a cavernous hollow
that sound travels more quickly?

Uninhibited by the clutter
of clever obstructions
distractions, approval, disapproval
these wasted acceptances
of a life that should have been enough
but somehow lacked that satisfying sense
of a full emptiness
at the edge of a severe courage

A voice grows in this round enclosure
a low growl
that vibrates in the bones
moving through red streams
toward the heart center
so used to feeding all but myself

and there
with the growl becoming louder
dark red-stained fingertips
reaching more boldly
into a spiral darkness
I am safe
I am whole
Here
I am contained inside a wild mercy.

Descent

Descent embodies darkness.
It is the moving away from the light
in order to take on the tasks of gestation
dissipation, and the reordering of a life
all at once.

Darkness is full
not the empty, fruitless void
we have been told it is.

It is ripe with potential.

It is also exacting, tiring, and hard work
to the mind that is always grasping
for rationality and timeliness.

But time and order, as we crave it
do not rule in the spaces
of descent and darkness.

A different kind of order takes over.

Spiraling
diving
dropping down into
releasing
tearing
coming apart...

these are the words and images
we sense about us
when we are nearing or experiencing
descent.

It can be so heavy
the journey of descent.
It is meant to be so.

And there are times
in the heavy darkness
that we may feel the temptation to run
screaming through those corridors
scanning the walls for the way out
feeling the cold stone surrounding us
thinking mournfully that this is looking less
like a wombspace for rebirth
than a tomb where nothing may stir
ever again.

In our fear and discouragement
we may come close
to ending the journey prematurely
and it is understandable.

It hurts: the stripping away.
It is uncomfortable: the nakedness we feel.
I know.
I travel these hallways regularly.

It does not get easier
because each descent is always new
and the passageways are formed
for our own specific shedding and rebirth.

My cave does not look like yours, dear one-
it looks like the me I need to leave behind
the me I need to transform.
And you know what yours looks like.

But we have been gifted along the journey
with tools to make this lightless pilgrimage
more sane.

Hold tight to them.

Only you can know what they are
and only you may use them.

They are oracles bearing words
that burrow deep into your psyche
spurring you on into hope
and the realization that
This Too Shall Pass.

They can anchor us
and help us stay in our body
when all we want to do is escape.

They remind us that the spirits are ever near.
We are not alone.
They make this journey with us
offering help along the way.

They are the call to the ancestors.
And they are the response we receive.

They summon us to the spaces of
communion
where we are reminded in dark moments
of our holy and necessary purpose.

It is this reminder
that keeps our aching feet on the path
our tired eyes looking forward
and our sore heart open
to the direction wisdom points out to us
despite the pain of descent.

To make use of the soul's tools
we must reach into the sacred earth
of our mother tongue
seeking a solace that is only found
in solitude.

This quiet inner prayer
becomes a dialogue
and we discover that we are speaking
with a truer self
a self who is courageous
in a way we yearn to be
in daylight hours.

It is there
in the hours of solitude and stillness
that we hear the soulspeaking voice
most clearly.

She listens to our words with a quiet
patience.
But do not mistake this for gentleness.

The healing medicines we need
are not always a soothing salve.
Sometimes they sting in the cleansing.

But you can know they are trustworthy.
May this knowledge keep you
when you have one foot out the door.

Unfailingly
it is there that we are shored up
restored, and encouraged
on the journey of descent
to whole-soul ways
newly born truths
and the deepening maturity
of a genuine personhood that ever calls out.

Grace

I have chosen an intrepid road.
Give me dirt-soaked soles and snaky roots
that merge with grace
on their journey to the sacred center
of all things.

And as I walk
stain my heart with the light of love
that in my wild flight
I not lose sight of my self
of the self in the Other
and the light in the Beloved.

Fill these hands with holy air
loaded with the heavy sense of purpose
that pulls me forward
as if tethered to my wrists
drawn to all life-giving things.

Speak kind and fierce
words of sight to my eyes
that the seeing of my soul
may grow larger
clearer
sharper
in the scouting of wild lands
and bordering seas.

A Homestead Heart

I will not be defeated by fear.
This way was made
by those who chose bravery.
I who follow in their wise steps
do not say "fearless" because I feel no terror.
Rather
I claim Fearless as my name
because I refuse
to do that thief of courage
any further honor
give to it any further power
pay it any further homage.

My heritage
is a millennium of brave hearts
and seeking minds
fierce-bodied women
forging life
from generations of dust
and wind-soaked frontiers.

I am the daughter of millions.
I am the mother of new truths.

These choices before me require nothing
less
than the honest looking-in
to the smoky soul spaces
and the settling-in
to the ready knowing within me.

It is there.
It has always been there.

Be brave, my heart.
Now is your time.

The Spirit Child

We are initiated into aboriginal, sacred
mysteries
when we enter new territories
take on burdens that may seem unbearable
and even when the soul itself feels to be
stolen
perhaps especially in that case.

It is interesting then
that something that has been taken from us
is described as being 'spirited away'.

In moments when we recognize violation
it is indeed as if the spirit has left us
the air gone out of our lungs
deflating and fatiguing body and mind.

We discover that the anguish of the theft
is, in itself, an initiation
into a greater depth
of self-discovery.

From that bereaved place
something is born in us
that strengthens and brightens
until the eyes are able to see the way ahead
more clearly.

The Spirit Child in us moves quickly
to retrieve the lost or stolen skin
returning it to us, so long deprived.

Beyond the reclaiming of the soul
the Spirit Child moves between the worlds
rooting us in the reality that requires plans
rules and limiting structures
and the creative, soulful flow that beckons
from far out at sea-
that deep blue green place
that is home.

We are flesh that must find a way
to live in both places.

In the most painful, skinless states
we will see a small, wavering flicker
that warms us with the knowledge
that something is coming
if we would be patient enough
to allow it to surface.

There is a powerful lesson to be gleaned
here
hidden inside the tears.

Reclaiming oneself
is the journey of returning home.

But we are meant for both worlds
and are given the task of the Spirit Child
to navigate back and forth
among these coastal shores and wooded hills
with equal skill in each terrain.

And there is always the comfort
that we are first and always meant
for the home places within us
and it is the promise of the soul
that the Spirit Child can bring us back.

Our pain and our persistence create an
alchemy
that summons the spirit.
Plans emerge, wisdom drops in
the soulskin appears.

Shapeshifting

Underneath the sleeping at the surface
there is a stirring that begins at the center
that reminds you of the days you roamed
the open spaces
prowled the wilder places
lived in freer lands.

A stirring that pulls you back
to the beginnings of you
to rocky outcroppings
hard packed earthen floors
and the fire lit cave
where you were dreamed into shape.

You came in the form of stars
that howled their way into bodies
of blood and bone and fur and teeth.

You were stalked
in the meadows
the forests
the plains
you were driven into the sea.

You emerged on the foam of waves
caught in the midst of buoyant seaweed
ropes
entangling each flailing limb
snarling your legs
with words
and the flame of living visions
that pulled and sucked at your toes
until at last
half-buried
in the demand of your dreams
you shifted shape again.

These dreams
that rooted you down
serpentine
sinuous
twining anchors
that fastened you to the center heat
molten spiraling coils
hardening bark skin
and an endless reaching
toward a waiting sky
and green leafy daydreams
of sap and spring
and bursting seeds.

And the stirring returned
as the days became short
the winter winds
carved the rock you became
from the wood you once were
hollowing out
the shape of a circle.

You've transformed once more.

You have become
the cave that gave you life
and watch
wiser
as new life begins again
at your center.

A warm glow fills the space
the stars have returned
a howling ensues.

She's come near.

Beautiful Broken Things

There is a rest in brokenness.
You lie on that hard ground
unable to function as you did before.

So you lie there.

There are no more shoulds
because the luxury of self recrimination
was taken from you when you fell
and broke to pieces on the earth below.

Cannot
doesn't matter now, either.

All that exists in this moment is What Is
Now.
This.

And there is beauty in the brokenness.

It is a beauty of constellations in the scars
of tides in the tears
the heat of fire in the bleeding of you.

In the abrupt quiet
that follows an unexpected injury
a sacred silence fills you.

And because there is nothing left in you
that can create, push, force, be, or drive into
there is a blessed empty space
to be filled by something other
than all the crazed and busy thinking
the manic achieving
the over-scheduled hours.

This blessed, beautiful brokenness
is the prayer that summons the spirit
calls forth the angels
lays us down gently.

In these seasons of humble brokenness
we are opened, utterly.

There is no protecting yourself here.
This is the stripping away
of ego-driven, striving conception.

Let there be grace.
Let there be mercy.
Allow the broken places to show you
their beautiful rest.

The broken stick on the forest floor
is the branch who earned her rest.
I bless the stick.
I bless the branch.
I bless the rest.

Bone Songs

I have come to believe
that a key element of sacredness
is uncovered in the difficulty we experience
while gathering its mystery to us.

As we journey through the dark night of the
soul
there are, in equal measures
confusion, pain and fear.

It is then that we are accompanied
by the old one
the gatherer of bones.
She walks at our side as we push on
through the dark.

She speaks to us of the roots
the bones of a thing.

She draws the eyes downward
below the surface, beneath the blood
to the central marrow where those red rivers
are born in secret.

It is in the bones of a thing
that our blood is pressed to flow
to move air to the hungry places.

The gatherer of bones reminds us
that it is these bones
that anchor us, that root us
in this incarnation
this flesh.

Inside the roots of any grief, of any struggle
resides a pilgrimage into deeper mysteries
deeper awareness, deeper understanding.

This is initiation
where we experience a compression
that hurts like hell
but that pushes and propels
the life force forward
into flow once more.

We may feel as though everything
has become sensitized
raw and aching,
exposed to a wild winter wind.

We may feel that our bones are far-flung
across a desert
thrown hard against rock
drowned in a churning river
sinking into silt and small stones
that weigh them down
never to be recovered.

Ah, but La Loba the old one
the gatherer of bones
seeks them out
this is what she does.

Pulling, yanking, retrieving them
one by one
from the mucky and hidden places
she sets them back in their proper order
and will begin the creation song once more.

And the singing may hurt
as flesh is woven over our bones.

But living blood must flow, that is its nature.

And so it must be reborn
in the center of us
at the root of us
where life takes hold in the bones.

The song is a compression
where bone meets heart
again and again in sharp thrusts.

LIVE!

it screams
and the scream is the song
that the old one sings.

The song is beautiful-not-beautiful in my
ears.

It sounds like the chaotic buzzing of flies
the cawing of carrion-eaters
and the deep boom of explosives
tearing the ground up
from underneath me.

But I am not being torn apart.

I am being woven together
in this very moment
by skilled hands and the shrewd eyes
of an ancient bone woman
who finds me again and again.

This is her promise
to our wild soul selves:
We will not be abandoned.
We will be found.
Every element will be invoked.
Every measure will be taken
in the healing of us.

La Loba will sing
over our bleached-out remains
until the blood flows once more.
Our howl will return to us
we will be embodied again.

This I know.

Home Truths

She's got dirt under her fingernails
that look like tiny black crescent moons.

She has stayed with me-
this failing woman
this struggling, wounded woman.

I know in my own body
the pain of her uncertainty
the shame that wants to lodge itself
deep into the skin
like a thorn
when it is discovered
that, in fact
she really isn't that brave after all.

Actually
given half a chance
she'd run screaming
in the opposite direction.

Her Strange Angels

But she'd know
the pain and the work would be there
just waiting to get in her face
once she arrived
to whatever destination
she thought might bring relief.

That's a home truth she picked up
along the road
the last time she ventured underground.

The scrapes from that journey
are still a bit tender
and she won't be forgetting
anytime soon.

She's sick to death
of trying to say anything beautifully
in her bid to survive.

She has finally begun to get into my skull
the understanding
that sometimes we learn in the lovely ways
but sometimes
the wisdom only appears in the weeping.

No pretty crystal teardrops
but heated sobs that steam
the kind that leave shoulders and necks
sore afterward
because it was work even to cry.

Another home truth lives here.

I know her frustration
in feeling so tired of saying
I'm sorry
for everything
to everyone.

She knows she dropped the ball
screwed it up, let you down
disappointed, surprised
shocked, angered...

She looks at me in private moments
and shrugs her shoulders.

I worry for her
I feel like I hate her at times
but actually
I love her
this very less than perfect woman.

This woman who is me
who I am still getting to know
who frightens me with her loud feelings
and comforts me inside strong solid arms.

Where I worry and fret
she isn't so concerned
with making her labor look effortless.

She is a believer in speaking only truths
and that would be nothing more
than a pretty lie.

It's sweaty, bloody work
that sucks every drop of self
into the alchemical pot
for the mixing of us.

This wounded woman is wise enough to
know
that it is her suffering
that will be the making of her.

This particular home truth has fangs.
It moves and writhes like a serpent in the gut
transforming even as it sheds
tightening skin
in the next cycle of growth.

It is inextricable from the psyche
once uncovered at last.

She is my catalyst.
She wakes me up to my authentic life.
She is heavy
dark stone that acts as anchor
grounding me to what is real
and what is healing.

She peels away the layers of pretense
exposing the raw real feelings I hide
and makes it so that I am forced to look
and choose my way honestly.

Her Strange Angels

She cuts through the fog of my confusion
and requires me to set aside
everybody else's plan, expectation, or
opinion
in favor of my own true north.

Looking up at me expectantly
from her seat on the ground
my dirty companion fixes me with a sad
smile
that beckons me to join her.

I give in at last
plopping down ungracefully.

There's a thousand other things
screaming for my attention
and I can hear their voices behind me
demanding a response.

I'll just ignore them awhile longer
and fill my hands with cool dirt
moving it around and through my fingertips.

I have digging to do.

Reclamation

We begin to understand, painfully
the work of reclamation that lies before us
We must repair our vessel
We must call forth the rains
The river must be restored
so we can navigate those waters once more.

We can return our own disturbed, ailing
lands
to healed, whole territories
through the ditch digging work of
reclamation.

If it is unlovely, if it stinks of decay
if it is ignored, and left to rot
until it is unrecognizable
even to our own eyes
this is where the work of reclamation
must begin.

It is not enough to declare
to decide to stand up and plant ourselves
at the boundary line of our true home.

There is the dredging of the river
the clearing out, the way-making
that must be done.

Things will never return
to their original state of being.

That time and those shapes are past.

There must be a new form
a different sort of wholeness
that did not exist before reclamation began.

It is often in the midst of our deepest despair
that feeling that all is lost
and we've done it
for good this time
that the skilled hands of reclamation
begin their secret work
along a narrow, winding way
deep within us.

We may feel we are crying, all the time.

But it is the weeping
that clears the film from our eyes.
It is the weeping
though we wonder if it will ever cease
that calls to the holy rains.

Beauty, we are equipped
for this necessary and sacred work.

Though we may have been captured
and parts of us sold off bit by bit
our treasures are not lost forever.

Reclamation is the work
of seeking out and repairing
those stolen parts of our self
and through patience and diligent labor
we can piece ourselves back together again.

The river waits for us
for our tears and our tempests.

And when the voice feels drowned out
in the flood of own tears
we can remember that it is our weeping
that fills the empty riverbed.

This is the very moment
our soul waters rise to carry us home.

Our shattered self has become a prism
and a new kind of whole is emerging.

Ripening

The voice you once thought lost
will return to you.

Do not be surprised when you realize
that her tone is deeper, richer, and a bit
wilder
than the voice you remembered.

She has traveled
through the belly of the underworld
and while you spent your nights
plotting escape from captivity
she seasoned
in the dark recesses of the earth.

Water

Water moves to her own womb sourced
rhythm
measuring time
in the ebb and flow of waves.

We are carried in those currents
whether or not we cooperate with them
acknowledge them
or even if we are unaware of them.

Our longing for the Wild Mother
begins in water
is nurtured there
and it is that same longing
that bears us away on twilight tides
at the end of all our days.

We learn the language of release
in tides that pull the shore further
from our grasp
and all our reasons and plans
along with the million grains of sand
that littered our path just a moment before.

Let go, they croon
Shhhhhh…it's not yours… let go.
This is step one in shapeshifting.

This is not merely a race
back to the center
where all things debris
are deposited and roiled
into new sea-made fragments.

The sea retreats to her homeland
weary of the journey
to the hard dirt packed lands
of the east and west
surrounding her always.

Only in the blue-black fathomless depths
are those waves and native deep sea
creatures
truly renewed in the undisturbed waters
of their own moveable motherland.

This letting go of the land
and all things solid, stable and certain
is the calling of sea
and all water-made creatures.

We are pulled by these tides into retreat.

Out to the open bowl of the sea
we are sung
a return and reminder of where we began
and where we must come home to
for healing, for rest, and the next steps
of wisdom
that funds our transformation
as soul selves, mermaids, women.

Women and water
are magical containers
of fluid truths
and the ingredients of creation
in all its forms.

In a constant state of gestation, labor and
birth
of things creative and critical
we run the risk of drying up and out-
a condition that can become terminal if left
untreated.

To retreat is both wise and necessary
to life.

Resist it though we may
the soul will have her way
with our body and mind
and the sea song will grow louder
in the rush of our blood
reminding us that we are always
ever
water first
and that must be honored.

To move away
to move back into
to back away from...
these intentional and purposeful
movements away
from our solid substantial commitments
are medicine
that the soul requires.

Given the right time and space
this intentional retreat
both soothes and saves the heart
from terminal despair
and reminds us of our true name
the one lost in the waves so long ago
we nearly forgot it.

So we press intentionally into retreat.

The waves sing the song of promise
and there is something
infinitely comforting
in the idea of breathing water
for a time
away from the heaviness of so much air
and more gravity.

Water has been rushing in my own ears
flooding my senses with the scent of salt
and the sound of selkies.

They are miles off the shore
barely visible to my eyes
but I can see them waving a familiar
sealskin
that reminds me
I misplaced mine somewhere.

It beckons to me… Come Home.

The skin is marked and gouged with scars
so I know it must be mine.

At The Precipice

You saw yourself as something small
didn't you?

Something insignificant and unworthy of
_____.

It was too big, too bright, too good to be
true.

Waiting for the bottom to fall out
haven't you now?

Too much, too far, too easy
too pleasurable to be

Real?
Attainable?
Get-attable?
Sustainable?

So.

And now here you are, Beauty.

Seated on prickles and butterfly wings
at the edge of a cliff
a strong wind at your back.

And your longing is to

just.
lean.
forward.

What happened?
Why the change?

Did something crack open suddenly?
Did you finally awaken
in the middle of the night
to your power, your promise, your path?

What spirit beckoned to you at dusk
in the clapping leaves
of evening breezes
reciting the destiny of the ages
into your ear?

What lightning strike has singed your soul?
What gods burned the sacred bush
in the cavernous reaches of your heart?

No, no
this was the trickle of erosion
I know.

A gradual gracing that touched you
in the private and public spaces of life
reaching into you and pulling you out
of yourself
long enough to see the bigger picture
the larger circle
the deeper well
waiting for you and your work.

And now you come to it:
Your passion, your words, your colors, your
thunderstruck voice.

It is only now
alone in the market
or surrounded by strangers on the train
you are recognizing
what you have known
to be your truth
for many a moon now.

It was a thousand little cuts
that brought you to your fearlessness
and a million small pleasures
that catalyzed your call to action.

This minute, yet requisite process
that moved through you
drip by solitary drip
until the accumulation
of every tear
and every shrug
and every single word
heard or spoken
became the herald
whose foreign voice you somehow knew
without understanding why
or when it came to be.

To lean forward into the wind
inside the container of perfect trust
this small but powerful movement
that becomes
a disruption of gratitudes
push, push, pushing their way
through the crowded room
of discontent and self-doubt
that holds you back from the gift
of freefalling grace
of such sweet wind in your face.

This beauty way
these wisdom paths that open slowly
These are precipice truths
revealing treasures
through mist and the unfurling petals of pain
there in the open air of possibility
fed by those who are unafraid to be bruised.

Your bravery, my love
has appeared inside the daily practice
of presence
that ritual ennobled
by a saturation of holy waters
inside tears that washed you
free of binding fears
and the holier dirt of struggle
that covered you utterly
in the fresh sacred soil
of rooted knowing.

Your ambivalence: a gift
that pulled you back to a safer distance
wrapped in stronger arms than yours
as eruptions intensified around you
those volcanic messengers
that screamed you awake
to your purpose moment to moment.

The blessed reprieves
the poetry of unasked for pleasures
the hundred songs of suffering
and the wetness of frustrated weeping
that streaked your hidden face
unaccustomed as you've been
to the nakedness of honesty.

These *all* brought you
to a Now moment of wings
Of wildness
Of wind
and the choice to lean in.

There is a surprise yet waiting, though.

Purpose-full falls into empty air
signal cellular shifts
and it's a new being you will become.

Losing so much mass
trading toes for talons
and a bird's wing rises
from the place where arms used to hide
that soft underbelly you were afraid to show
others.

She is clawing and cawing her way free
inside you
pushing out of your chest, your eyes
your mouth
until all that is left of you
is feathers
and a fierce need to hunt
for all the promises left behind
in the years abandoned to fear
just waiting to be reclaimed.

Oracles

This wildish instinct self
the one who orders me to
LEAP
try
risk
she is unconcerned with my petty fears
or others' petty opinions.

She rises up
at precisely the perfect moment
and says precisely the perfect words
needing to be said
when I begin shivering inside my skin.

Those words flood me when I am alone
an inner dialogue that builds me up
to a courage needed
for new feet treading wild land.

You are mine.
And I take care of what is Mine.

They're raw, unapologetic
red and smoke and salt.

They look me square in the eye
daring me to look away
holding my shoulders in a vise grip
commanding my attention.

Like the sweetness that spoke itself
earlier in my heart
I receive these new words
flooded up, righteous, final, firm, rooted
establishing themselves around me
like concrete pillars
encasing some sacred space
where gods drink their fill
and oracles appear.

Guardians

The wild thing in us
the beast that is wholly untamed
holy in her movement
prowls around lapping at wisdom
like water
and feeding in places
where good views are assured.

Like any wild thing
she will be hell to catch unawares.

I am glad for this
so very glad.

Even in the throes of deep fatigue
it is comforting to know
that our wild soul is ever on the lookout.

The Witness

And there comes a time when you have to
say the truth words of your life.
To bear witness of your Self.

There are two lives too many of us live:
the life shown carefully to the world
and our real one.

In this real life of mine
I will no longer ignore
the thousand million seconds
of waste
of wandering
pacing
waiting or weeping.

I cannot pretend or wish
these unbeautiful moments away.

These bereft moments
the abandoned seconds and hours and days
are part of the story, and must be witnessed
as the beautiful is witnessed
with grace
with a holy nod of acknowledgement
with respect for the struggle.

I want to recognize each moment
as a glowing ember
a divine gift
that is witnessed even when I turn away
from the ugliness.

And there is a witness to each moment
a sacred scribe who takes notice
of our every single tear.

Who takes notice of us.

The true us.

The private, secret, longing
wanton us.

The us we show no one
least of all ourselves
for fear of rejection.

For shame.

There is a witness.

Her message is ever the same
and her fluid truth moves slowly
in to the body
releasing the breath
opening the spaces that were bound up
carefully filling the questing and seeking
places
with answers that are less
specific
than they are
real.

We must be intrepid souls
because this way to wisdom
is an uncut path in the dark, love.

There are only
unpredictable outcomes
daily chores
and glimpses into glory
and it may be that those glories
sustain our hearts
on the journey toward Wholeness.

But it is the ditch digging work of everyday
that moves us forward into elder wisdom
and compassion for self and others.

It's only Life.
It's only everything you've ever wanted
and feared
and hidden from
and raced after with all your might.

The boring, bloody mess of our days
are not subservient
to the holy work of transcendent creation.

They are creation.

And each act of creation is witnessed.

Breathed upon
filled to the brim
with some profound pneuma
that directs our steps…
we continue on.

And we are loved.
And we are seen.
Witnessed.

Beauty, allow the okays.

Allow the alrights
the ughs and sighs
the lumps in the throat
and the tears spilling over shiny lids
that are working so hard
to restrain your own flood of feeling.

Let the chin have her quiver
the lips their tremble
let the heart run her race
and allow the hands their shaking.

These are the other side of the ecstatic
experience.

You sought the epiphanies
and with them comes the shadow.

There is no flow without the ebb
and the ebb we must all observe
inside ourselves
inside the process.

And yet, there is a witness.

No moment, no matter how mundane
goes unnoticed.
This life does not go by unnoticed.

The beautiful moments
the ugly
and the four billion others within that
spectrum between communion with the
Divine
and fallen-flat-on-my-face-failure.

Our witness collects every breath
every attempt is sacred
every scar vulnerable to her hands.

She holds them all carefully
filing each away in a holy archive.

Each moment and every feeling
EXISTS
therefore it has merit
value
the pneuma of divine life-right.

She speaks into our left ear
that each dip and dive
is as equally holy in its curvature
as the breakthroughs into bright light.

There is no flow without the ebb
and it is the ebb we must ride back in
straight to the source of all things.

Through those journeys into the dark
the ugly, the repetitive have tos
that sometimes feel like filmy water
that is tossed on soulfires
there is a witness.

The most insignificant parts and pieces of us
these throw-away moments
have become holy
because they have been seen
by our soulself witness within.

This is the sacred nature of discarded things.

This is the holiness of gathered tasks
foregone conclusions
wasted opportunities
and the gall of ill-equipped and {as yet}
undisciplined feet
over hard packed earth.

There she is again.
Our Witness-Self.
She Who Hears.
She Who Sees.

Can you feel her near?
You are not invisible, brightling.
You are seen by this witness.

Your story is the story of ten thousand
who came before you
but your link on this ancient chain
is unique
fashioned by elder hands
who stand as witnesses
to your own creation
your own handiwork
your own matter of soul.

The terrain of your life
undulates with the complex and varying
patterns of light
that can sometimes play tricks on the eye.

This great work
that is your life
is not a portrait.

We are the wild yearning
of an untamed landscape
lush with the cycles of life, death
and the many stages of growth and decay
in that marshy middle land.

And every stage, every cycle, every moment
is witnessed.
Matters.
And to Matter, is to be Matered
is to be Mothered.

We are mothered.
Every moment, each ebb, every dip, dive,
fall, stumble and shriek is Mothered.
Held to a great, soft bosom
and nurtured to wholeness once more.

Born up from underneath by the dark ground
witnessed in the soil.

Mothered
by the Rememberer of Time Before Time
Keeper of All Things
Transformed and Reborn.

Beloved, these moments
these dark shadows that haunt us
in the ebb of things
they are no less precious
simply because they are unlovely.

For now, just for this little space
let it be enough that these feelings
these uncomfortable places
and the unbeautiful moments
are part of the same circle
the infinite and ever turning cycle
that comprises the holy
the sacred, secret ways of wisdom.

We are witnessed in grace.
We are witnessed unto healing.

She

She's come near again.

She is ever the center.
The fluid beginning, middle and end
The source and the leaving behind
of worn out ways that precede
newness of thought
of shiny starts and fresh earth
under our fingernails and feet.

She sees us at our worst
and smiles her luminous smile anyway.
She is our wild yearning toward HOME
the soul-whisperer.

She stands there in the shadow of the tree
watching all the floundering
calmly standing her ground
amidst tromping fits of fear, failure and
shame.

She is the still point
the pivot-point
the ground beneath dirty feet
care-taking each sacred second.

She lies inside our inner waters.

She is the Acknowledger
the One Who Validates
every breath
every struggle
every tear and every drop
of sweat and blood shed.

She is the container
the wish-hearer
the other side of the line.

She is the vacuum that fills itself up.
She does not discriminate among wildlings
for we are all samesoul
of a kindred and fierce source point.

She is the one who stands inside the
doorway
unconcerned with insults
or petitions to, Look away! I am unclean!

She is the eye that sees into the darkness.

She cuts through the blackness of fright
with precision
and sees ALL of it – down to the bone
the blood, the stink and swell
of things left unsaid, undone, unfinished.

She is the body of evidence
where they said none could be found
and She is the finger in the sand
separating the Wills from the Did-Nots
the Fears from the Fear-Nots
the Past, the Now and the Could-Be's
if you'd only wake up
and see who SEES you
in perfect clarity.

She is the bearer and bringer of soul
and the funnel of all things wise and sacred.

She is the Secret Keeper
the advocate
for all of us unworthy, indefensible,
untamed illogical, irrational and feral-eyed.

She is the courier
of our every darkening moment
carrying each thought, glimpse and dirty
corner
into safety
succoring us to trust again.

We are not hers only when we behave
as the fresh faced wildlings she adores
but hers when the lights fade away
when the holy water has turned tepid at last
the incense burns out
the food spoils
the muscles atrophy from mis or disuse
when the balance is lost
and the cavernous in us collapses.

Deathing

Come to me, ending.

Remind me
you are rebirth
shedding her skin,
making room
for new blood,
new veins,
new breath.

In the Belly

We yearn toward the light.
It is yearning that keeps our feet on the path
when the dark threatens to overtake our
hearts
and we feel faint with dread
and soul-numbing fatigue.

But before the birth time
the greening, leafing of spring and warmth
there is the time in the belly of a thing.

It's a strange feeling
drifting in a reality that is completely
foreign
destabilized and freefalling into the
unknown
while simultaneously contained
within a process entirely out of known
control.

At times thrilling and warm
Sometimes a keen sense of loss
Of anxiety- around the great unknowns to
come
the changes, the inevitable altering.

156

This is more than cosmetic change
at the surface.

The very pattern
of the weave of life
as it has been understood
is moving through a transformation
that will leave us forever marked.

This is initiation.
The dirty work.
The scraping away of old flesh
to make way for something
new, larger, louder, brighter.

Bleeding, opening, cracking ground
to make way for new shoots to spring up.
Surrendering to an unknown outcome
because there is
truly
no going back.

And because even if I could at this point,
I wouldn't.

So initiation is a door
I humbly, if timidly
walk through of my own accord.
I am not forced.

Initiation is intrinsically cleansing.

It is the most basic of purifications
played out in profound measure
for the stretching of us.

Can you feel the pulling
at every end, beloved?
It always begins in the belly.

I fidget, I squirm, I resist, I curse
and finally...
I collapse
surrendering to the process
of this birth before birth.

Moving through that birth canal is a team
effort.
The child struggles toward the light
turning this way and that
compressing and bending limbs and even
bone to fit.

The familiar warmth of amniotic fluid
filling the soon to be airway
is pushed away
in this labor toward the light.

All this happening in the belly
and below.

This is initiation
moving in the belly.

Together. We.
Our mind and our soul.
Our experience and our Self.

We who are today
and our potential
fighting for life
and clawing toward breath.

It is as much a taking away
as it is a giving in to.

The emptying that comes
before the filling up
and the aching arms that were pleasantly full
of the weight of all that was
now required to grow accustomed
to air and possibility.

We accumulate knowledge, practices
and truths
that serve us well.
Until they don't.
We outgrow them.

They must move through us
out, onward and away from us
to new hearts waiting for them
as others travel toward us
waiting for us to invite them in
and choose the initiation
that will allow us
to understand their language.

They arrive in the belly first.

A clenching in the gut
of faint but definite recognition.

Oh, there you are!
we hear ourselves say
I was wondering when you would arrive…

Our mind tricks us into believing
there is security in the known.

If we know it, if it feels familiar
if we are used to its weight and heat
it must be truth and true for us
always.

But this is false, and holds us back
from the growth we are meant for.

It stalls the birthing process
stopping it dead in its tracks.

Refusing initiation in any form
when it appears to us
in the secret moments
the pained silences
the raging grief or quiet loss
of a thing, person, or idea
is certain death to our evolution
at some point along the way.

There must be movement toward the light
from the belly place of a thing.

Where life stirs in secret darkness
before it can be born.
Preparation looks as much like clearing out
as it does adding to.

This is more than a quaint decluttering.
This is cleansing on a life-changing scale.
It cuts to the bone.

And it's time.
Time to let go of what used to serve us
that we are past now.
Time to hold ourselves accountable
to the deeper truths
that have been growing
in strength
in the belly.

Maps

What is familiar
what is known
is not better
where abundant life is available.

To cross that chasm
to leap that imposing divide
into an abundant spring
requires a brave initiate
and the map only you can read.

It was written for no one else.

Amputations

There is a vast ocean of difference
between freeing oneself from a trap
and running from a life-saving amputation.

Your blessing
and your challenge
is that you know in your guts
which it is.

Surrender

To willingly relinquish one's control
one's idea of how it should be
to lay down all the tools
and weaponry
that struggles to keep inevitability at bay.

But not powerless.

She is the sister whose offered hand
we reluctantly take
walking toward the underground tunnel
we didn't know existed.

The Tunnel of The Way.
The Way you Did Not Know.
The Way of Initiation.
The Way of Death and Rebirth.
The Way of Unexpected Wholeness
and Startling Truth.

Surrender brings you
and shows you the way.

You are led, barefoot and bleeding
through the dark of your soul
in the bewilderment of your heart
to a place where cool earth waits.

Surrender you sister
is a marvelously gifted and expert guide.

Thought she carries a sword
in the hand at her side
do not be alarmed.

She will care for you here.

Whatever is cut
hacked
and bleeding in you
will begin the mending
remembering process of healing
in Surrender's earthen home below.

You will stay with her awhile.
For many days
weeks
perhaps months.
You will maybe stay longer.

Once the time is right, though
you will return above ground
 to the leaves and the winds
and the yellow sunlight.

You may have trouble recognizing yourself
as well as others.

Your ears, eyes and nose changed
while you were underground.

Your sight softened in the darkness so long.

Your hearing magnified
within your skull and throat
bringing the pattering steps of mice
to your consciousness
as the thud and thwack of big things
dark and powerful things prowling the night.

And your sense of smell sharpened
growing so accustomed to the moist soil
beneath your feet
and the scent of woody roots
above your head.

Surrender has given you gifts:

gifts used in the night
where the brightest light is bestowed
by the moon.

Surrender has shown you
the greatest wisdom to be found
 in the silent places
where no voice is heard
for no voice is needed.

And though, in the beginning
you felt such deep sorrow
in your unbidden silence
and it's great, pervasive
relentless progress
taking over every part of you -
you have come to see
that silence is yet another sister
teaching you great and secret things
giving you great and holy gifts.

Gratitudes

As each new day has come
small pleasures
have entered through my windows
and padded gently across my floors
whispering gratitudes
that become promises of joy.

Temenos

A woman's life
is a study in season-ing.
Both her body
and her psyche
live each in turn
in and out
through and around
every mood, need, and longing
that finds her, ready or not as she may be.

Mother Dust looks on our days with ageless
eyes.
To become dust is to lie fallow
that lovely word
~ fallow ~
it drips and falls off my tongue
reminding me that the word
{allow}
sits inside.

The terrain of undisturbed land is holy.
She lies in wait, seasoning
for us.

Such land is a sacred space
set aside for divine use.
The Greeks had a word for such a place -
temenos.

All my nutrients are spent.
I have grown many things
without resting.
There is nothing left right now
and that is as it should be.

A quiet empty space
takes up the opening
in my body.
I have room now
to sit still inside
warm autumn earth
that waits her turn.

I am becoming
a land undisturbed
terrain set aside for divine purpose
temenos.

Roots of living things
used up in me
are dissolving into soil
that will feed something new
later.

Under my surface
I can feel a throbbing
pulsing vibration
gathering at my center.
I am saving up
these beautiful moments
like one stores seeds
for a future garden.
They are food
that is nourishing
my intentional inaction.

There is time yet.

DayDreams

Let these dreams
become my day
setting stardust footprints
into my kitchen
baking honeyed bread
that heals
even as
it delights.

May it Be.

Invocation

My Mother is a bursting moon.
She rises through the trees
to remind me that it does not matter
that I forgot Her-
She remembered me.
She re-members me
and I am made whole.

She sings me to sleep
through the rushing of winds
and the pelting rains that tinkle
against my back door
like fingernails tap, tap, tapping...
let me in, She whispers.

She speaks to me through the words
on the page I am reading-
I can hear Her voice narrating
Her very own story- my story
which is Hers: revised, revisited
re-incarnated through my own trials
my own tears, my own voice.

I am not alone
I am ever alone
holding the paradox
Everywoman holds every day.
There is no hurry.
There is no rush.
Everything in its own time.
I can simply sit in this space
and allow what must, to surface.

What must be is carried by its own force,
and nothing I do will increase its pace
nor prevent its arrival. It will be, or not
as it must.
The bursting Mother Moon must rise
and She will rise, and She will rise.

She rises within me through the tides
through the wave
through the dappling sunlight
the steam off the road.

She is the rock I can lean on
and the rock in my gut
the warning pitch that rings in my ears.
I make my altars to Her, and dismantle them
in turn.
Nothing stays the same.

She is the beauty of a black-headed Towhee
sitting on a fence post
red-eyed and song filled.
She is the falcon swooping down for the kill
red-eyes in Her sights, razor precision
in Her timing.
She is both Life and Death
and the spaces in between
the spaces of the last gasp
the final sigh
the long exhale before the rest.

She is all these things, my Mother
my Grandmother, my sister, my Self.

She is the haunting in the harp
and the flying in the hair.
She is the Strangled One who lived
to grow new vocal chords
and now uses them
to shriek Herself awake again.
Her song is lusty, loud and raucous.

She is Celtic, red-haired, and fiery.
She is African, Egyptian, Sumerian
Black, dark as midnight
wandering the city streets
in search of Her beloved.
She is many nationalities;
she is them all, and none of them at all.

And now my Mother transforms Herself
again.
Not only my Mother?
No, no..
She is so much more.

She is the Great One
Queen of Heaven
Lady Owl
Wisdom Incarnate
Goddess Divine
Grandmother of all ages
Keeper of the Flame
Holy Chalice
Womb of All Creation.

She is the many names
the holy faces
the sacred spaces
that free us
feel us
set us apart and call us together.

I bow.
even as I bow
I rise.

make holy this space.

Come, Spirit.

- NOTES -

Her Strange Angels

- NOTES -